D0758234

ALSO BY JIM POWELL

It Was Fever That Made the World

The Poetry of Sappho

SUBSTRATE

SUBSTRATE

JIM POWELL

PANTHEON BOOKS

New York

Pantheon Books and colophon are registered trademarks
of Random House, Inc.

Photographs courtesy of Dan Jones, Rinske Blok,
Thad Zajdowicz, and Amy Hill.

Library of Congress Cataloging-in-Publication Data
Powell, Jim
Substrate / Jim Powell.
p. cm.
ISBN 978-0-307-37788-3
I. Title.
PS3566.O8323S83   2009
811'.54—dc22   2008042272

www.pantheonbooks.com
Printed in the United States of America
First Edition
2 4 6 8 9 7 5 3 1

To Carlo Anceschi

CONTENTS

HABITAT

TIMON OF PHLIUS:
IN THE MUSES' BIRDCAGE

SUBSTRATE

SUBSTRATE

HABITAT

THE RESURRECTION OF THE BODY

Naked as the day they were born the first time
the newly resurrected blink awake wide-eyed and caper
innocent under heaven
in the final clarity of eternal everyday
like nudists without tennis shoes, unstartled

to resume bodies homely as the first,
lumpish and pointy elbowed, adult but not worn, like a loved coat
remade, a perfect fit
comfortable as an animal, an animal with a soul at home
entirely instinct with uncareful grace

the sting of seasons sated at the feast
where every head is numbered pleasure's instrument and slave
to pain—luck's buried hook
and fatal barb of risk—blunted this time, lost in the blast
this morning from the horn of Israfel.

RATES OF COMBUSTION

The air thins and clears
above eight thousand feet and distances
draw nearer: a silver pine snag
falls in the forest and over decades
disintegrates

as layer under layer
the rings of yearly growth break down in fragments,
the fat years and the lean,
fissure and crumble slowly inward
toward heartwood

which also crumbles, fracturing
beneath the pry and wedge of ice and insects,
snow, sunlight, rain,
the slow combustion of decay,
till all that's left

where the thick trunk lay
is a long strip of wood chips making a path
through the encroaching brush,
a strew of cubic segments the size
of finger bones,

the ridges of the grain
still visible on their striated faces
of burnished muted copper.
Come evening, a fading bed
of coals gives back

that brazen tarnished glow
below a grill of gaping rainbow trout
—the trout we feast on fattened
on mosquitoes that swarm at dusk
to feed on us.

HABITAT

Down the botanical garden's terraced slope
following where the path
led us among tagged specimens
assembled in neat plots
by family

and ecosystem, local plants and exotics
—even a young sequoia
from my native California—
each with its skirt of shade
underneath

gathered close in the solstice midday heat,
with sometimes a single leaf
in outline emerging from the tangled
mass of shadows cast
on the level dust,

its boundary describing the unique
silhouette peculiar
to its kind, and all the leaves above
outspread, reveling
in the common sunshine . . .

we strayed into a cool alcove, lingering
where the pharmacopoeia
detained us—ephedra, belladonna,
one small gray-barked tree
without a label,

a glossy red-orange globe on a long stem
smooth as a persimmon
suspended from a skinny branch
head high, a tin sign
enameled white

hanging on a silver chain beside it
with prim black lettering:
VELENO   NON TOCCARE.
Further on, where the slope
flattens out

and widens as the field sweeps gently down
to meet the towering
medieval wall—a sprawling acre
of tall grass and wildflowers,
thistles, vines,

undifferentiated pagan weeds
promiscuously nestled
against the fortification's brickwork,
the whole expanse of ground
let run wild

as if the circuit of the city wall
were a permeable membrane
admitting the wilderness inside,
wild and tame inter-
penetrating,

this city's trust in its identity
secure enough to allow
its opposite a place and share.
Just so, the visitor
who climbs slowly

back from the outskirts along narrow lanes
of sun-warmed brick emerging
into Il Campo senses the spreading
plaza's vast expanse
widen around him

the way a mountain meadow greets a hiker
in the wilderness who follows
the thin stripe of a trail through forest
shadows when suddenly
a clearing opens

and gathers him into the broad embrace
of high altitude
cerulean. But ah, Siena,
you are luckiest in the root
and stem whence

your hospitality flowers: each and all
your children trust that within
the encircling shelter of your wall
they will always have a place
at the table, a bed.

FIRST LIGHT

Graying chest hair emerging from his apron top in tufts
dusted with a snow of flour
above the swelling rondure of his oven belly,
sleeves rolled, arms folded, at ease on the porch steps
outside the back door of the bakery

in the lively air of the early hour taking a break
while the bread cools on racks inside
and a breeze picks up off the bay: the mist lifts
and the swarming dust of starlight reappears,
the constellations that were given names

beside the hive-domed ovens of Chaldea and of Ur—
near first light, thick arms cradling rolls
and crusty loaves, a gift for late-returning revelers,
for the derelict who washes in the creek
under the bridge his daily bread at daybreak.

EXPOSURE

The lion still rules the barranca

A doe and a pair of yearlings
detach from the shadow of the cliffs
and edge into the open
knees whispering through grass like wisps of tule fog
adrift in the starlit meadow

spectral silhouettes
ashimmer gliding warily creekward
they keep close to covert
yet where the bright thread of the path divides the clearing
one by one cross over

the exposed ground and wait
on the other side, mule ears cocked,
till he joins them and they vanish
into darkness behind the wide rack of the antlers, not hurrying
and not lingering.

PYRAMID SCHEME

Crone,
old meat,
once, this town was your home;
now you're living on the street.
The bottom line has put you there to rot.

You can't
pay the rent.
Every seven years
it doubles. Now shelter is too dear
for you, since who you are is what you've got.

It takes
six weeks to build
a cabin, six months to make
a house, but thirty years won't pay
for either, the banker and the landlord say,

so nightly
in TV dreams
the pyramid of paper
mounts in piles, it gets a purchase
on your back and towers and sprawls and sags

till what
you've got is what
you are—your family
's gone, the neighbors all rank strangers:
a shopping cart of newspapers and rags.

Crone,
caryatid
broken under your stone,
the full weight of the pyramid
crushes down on your shoulders anonymous as brick.

SOVEREIGNTY

The child riding his father's shoulders
above the crowd
looks down into the whirl of faces swimming at his knees,
king of the world
in his own mind:

at each turn alternate destinies
invite his liking;
he gapes meanwhile, and holds tight, safe on the charmed brink of
        childhood,
a bubble clinging
at the fall's lip,

delighting to be thus elevated.
Later, learning
to carry his own weight on solid ground he will denounce
the idols riding
his father's back,

curse naked king and paper crown
to make his way,
still not noticing how his choices begin to overtake him,
the water rising
at his heels.

And what if, his father's age, hearing
his own son
on his shoulders laughing in his blind spot he starts to glimpse
amid the hazard
of stray blows

like a face returning in a dream
the emerging features
of the fate that took him captive—sovereign, indelible:
suppose he finds
the means to climb

from the staining flood of self to see
the circle whole
and know he is what he's become as the weight bears him down
now will he
learn mercy?

THE SEAMSTRESS

Dia De Los Muertos

Knelt in the middle of the kitchen floor at midnight
there's only so much you can do to mend the skeleton
spread-eagled on the linoleum
painted in faded Day-Glo
on a black leotard:

the fabric stretches over time, the fibers strain
and give and never spring back all the way. Needle and thread
stitch up the raveled sleeve, a sponge
blots fresh florescence
onto spine and ribcage

but light leaks through the brittle weave, the needle's eye
grows dimmer, the grasp less sure, and joints ache on the cold floor
down again on hands and knees
to see the kindergartners
dance in the bones of the ancestors.

MIMESIS

A violet, a forget-me-not,
ruby magenta and baby blue
upright in an inch of water
in a glass creamer
the shape of a milk can.

She dips the brush in and rinses
wipes the tip on the pitcher's lip
adds red gingerly to the mix.
On the bare page
petal adjoining petal

a second pair of flowers
takes shape under her rapid hand—
a tiny woman bundled in woolens,
at her tweed elbow
her little sister's grandchild

feet dangling in midair
between the leaves of her kitchen table.
The water darkens around the stems
as she paints, drifting
filaments of stain

trail out clouds unfurling
upside down in a water sky
ruby magenta and baby blue
a violet,
a forget-me-not.

SEMPERVIRENS IN WINTER

Those lumpish mounds of dead leaves
huddled along the back fence are the blackberries
that overran the yard—five of us took all day
with hoe and shovel
gloves and machete

cutting them back last spring
to plant this garden and look: everything is puddles
and dissolution—borders breached, eroded beds,
the bean-row furrows
obliterated.

The tree stump in the middle
is old growth redwood cut knee high last century.
Its upper branches shaded all this ground and now
its broad girth serves
as garden altar:

the rain slick surface glistens
pocked by the downpour pooling in the weathered grooves
of its annual rings. Each year it sprouts back
another chaplet
of sapling shoots.

HUMAN

The Grizzly is extinct in California
except on the state flag
exterminated by American settlers
with baits of sponge congealed in bacon grease
that, once swallowed, blocked

the animal's digestion lethally
as they expanded, leaving
his habitat for mines and cattle ranches;
orchards and vineyards; malls and subdivisions,
factories, schools and prisons.

Before the Christian missionaries came
the aborigines
practiced coexistence with the bears
and there were one or two in every tribe
whose maiming showed the cost

of stubbornness or of misunderstanding.
The Californios
harassed them from their settlements and on holidays
would rope and tie one to a bull and watch them
fight it out for sport.

Then, after the Gold Rush, Yankee craft devised
the ultimate solution.

The California Black Bear in the wild
contrastingly aloof avoids human
contact and survives.

A VICTORIAN CONNOISSEUR OF SUNSETS

Contemplating the first smog
Ruskin thought it the lost souls
of the French dead
blowing across the Channel
from Paris where the Commune's last defenders fell

back fighting, driven through Père-Lachaise
from grave to grave in a meager drizzle:
starved workingmen,
beggars and country boys,
no one that counted, stumbling against the crowded costly

monuments in the failing light,
ricochets pocking the marble cheeks
of cherubim
and putti, bad art perched
at all four corners of massive family vaults in attitudes

of stony sorrow above their heads
as they fell together hand
to hand, enemies
dying in a single grave
for the brotherhood of man: their blood thinned with rain

water trickling down the grooves
of the lettering in the stones.
Those who surrendered
were lined up against
the cemetery's eastern corner wall and shot,

the mitrailleuses' impassive
regularity spattering
the summer grass
with gore and plaster. "The season
of revolutions now past, the red and black banners

no longer billow from the towers
of Notre Dame; yet the very spirits
of the air have sickened,
thickening with the exhalations
of the infected earth, and the sunsets run with fire and blood."

TEMPERAMENT

When the hammer blow of the hydraulic ram
slammed down on its head
to drive it square in the square hole
through the tie plate
anchoring rail to crosstie

a minute imperfection on one edge
of this steel spike snagged
on the lip of the aperture—
recalcitrant;
obstinate—and the ram's force

wrenched it awry. It skewed and twisted, jammed
the gears of the machine,
seized up the works. Unwedged, extracted,
tempered steel clawed
and dented, bent improbably,

it was cast aside on the crushed rock
ballast bed where I found it
and brought it home, cold in the hand.
Now it lies
on this page for a paperweight.

THE DOUBLE ALTAR ON PINE RIDGE

All this country is prone to burn, the chaparral-clad upper slopes
where the brink of Big Sur canyon plunges
toward the headwaters of its tributaries,
the rumpled mantle of scrub oak and brush
that hugs the shoulders and precipitous southern flanks

of the ridges trending down the coast in undulating folds,
manzanita, toyon, ceanothus, chamise,
evergreen shrubs with stubby needles, hard leaves,
waxy faces and dull undersides
for the torrid rainless summers: September lightning fires

draft up the steep ravines, their volatile oils vaporize and explode
thicket by thicket in roiling sheets of flame.
Once in twenty years it burns for days.
After the first rains in February
a flush of forbs and grasses overspreads the ashes

with rank growth where the soil burnt clear of shade lies reexposed
        to daylight.
By June ground squirrels will be numerous
and sleek from foraging its luxuriance
and, the April after, coyote litters large,
glossy pups on point in the lank weeds hunting ground squirrels

and on the knob above the spring hungry eaglets in the nest.
Higher, on the summit's landward peak
a careful circle of small rocks encloses
yucca, yerba santa, sage, live oak,
at the center a fire ring facing west, hearthstone

overlooking the immense hump of the opalescent Pacific Ocean.
Lodged in the waist-high cairn on the seaward crest
a spindly cedar fragment points true north.
At the tip of a wand tied with blue thread
three feathers flutter, invisible at any distance.

THE WRECK OF THE *PSYCHE*

Decks awash
cabin flooded
waves slapping at her hatchway
this little sloop
parted her mooring in the storm

and went adrift
driven broadside
against the other shore and foundered
stuck fast in bay mud
lashed for salvage alongside the jetty

mast akilter:
scavengers stripped
jib and bowsprit impromptu.
At high tide
entirely submerged her milky specter

filters upward.
Downward, daylight
penetrates a porthole
underwater
wallowing inside her cabin

where tidal flux
and salt commence
the slow dispersal of her remnants,
the cold ebb fingering
capsized memorabilia.

VERNACULAR

The long back of a tall man by firelight,
bony-shouldered, gray-ponytailed,
sarcastic T-shirt faded, jeans patched at the butt, embroidered, frayed,
holding a *guitarrón* customized as a four-string bass
like a Bug souped up with a Ferrari engine:

Bent above it, he cups its round wood belly
to his flat belly like a spoon
and leans into each phrase so that it issues from his solar plexus
as he pushes, birthing melody into the night air outward
from the fire ring under the great oaks' titanic branches.

His notes rise among the flickering limbs,
the strum and pluck of two guitars,
fiddle, harmonica, goatskinned *djembe,* and mix with the crickets'
        chirruping
in crisp October starlight across the grassy mountainside,
the bass sounding the fundamentals under all,

the foundation of the firmament of harmony
and discord, rhythm and inflection,
whose edifice encompasses and overshadows all dominion
within the round wood belly of an instrument, and there must be
room enough inside it to have so ripe a tone.

GHOST DANCE WITCH HUNT BLUES

Drove all night, the six of us
free for the weekend
barely cresting Pacheco Pass at dusk
sailed down the interstate
taking turns at the wheel

south through the valley out into the desert
lay down to rest and
woke, sleeping bags inflated, the dawn wind
flinging grit in our faces—
danced both days past

exhaustion giddy with the music
and the company, the motion
and the potions, the chalice and the vial:
late Sunday driving back,
a glow on the horizon

brightened at our approach, a prison,
another new one,
fences topped with spirals of razor wire
craning on all sides
relentless illumination

a false day abolishing shadow,
nowhere to hide,
no room to move. We shrank back, huddled close
inside the van's narrow
darkness and hurried on.

QUILL

for Larry Levis

inter odoratum lauri nemus

The Snowy Egret is a nervous bird.
Men coveted his plumes for ladies' Sunday hats
and hunted them to rarity
and now he is shy
and will not let you come too close.

He wobbles on one leg not far from shore,
the other agitates the bottom silt, all black
his rapier bill stabs dislodged bugs
as they swim upward
wavering into his reflection.

The inky water hides his yellow feet
that stir what rises toward the surface invisibly.
He never misses. It's his one trick,
his livelihood,
his niche. And so far he is not extinct.

CONSOLATION TO A DANCER

You cut your hair in mourning, your pride, that fully
touched your butt, a veil of cinnamon
fanned out whirling around your pirouettes,
its flag unfurling greetings to the wind
lifting our spirits on the pulse of trance—
and it will grow as long again and longer
before the ache of missing him is quiet
whose music took us where, the Sufis say,
dancing is to meet a god halfway.
We will not hear his living hand again
and now his music is entirely ours,
committed to the keeping of our care
for consolation, therapy and bliss,
and our feet know the way to climb its ladder.

in memory of Jerry Garcia

VENERY

Antelope flesh
is only succulent
if the animal
dies at ease:
muscle recently exerted
and drenched in adrenaline
tastes sour.
Besides, a bounding
pronghorn is almost
impossible to hit,
while no stealth
suffices to permit
approach within rifle shot
before they scare.

To hunt pronghorn
sit hidden in tall grass
distant but visible
to the herd, tie
a rag to a stick, raise and flutter it
above your blind till one
looks up.
Pause for grazing

to resume, and repeat.
Once they are drifting toward you
choose, and wait
for the tan strip to appear
between the two white blazes
on her throat.

ANCESTRAL TUMULUS

Daggers, broadswords, halberds, battle-axes,
shields, helmets, scabbard parts and buckles, spearheads,
manacles, necklaces, wine jars, war trumpets,
wagon, chariot and harness fittings,
armor and heraldic metalwork

entombed in wooden mortuary houses
under earthen mounds with severed skulls
of conquered enemies fashioned into goblets
ready beside the skeleton of the lord
seated in his vehicle of prestige

disassembled for passage to the next world
the godlike male, all drinking fighting man
surrounded by his concubines and servants
and strangled children to keep him company
across this threshold, and coins, thousands of coins.

AN ORACLE MADRONE

No plants grow
within the shadow of the vast madrone
because its bedded leaves exude
a chemical that poisons them
before they sprout.

In late September
band-tailed pigeons in antic flocks descend
to gorge on the red-orange berries clustered
shining among the upper branches
and strip them bare.

Toward nightfall
they wheel and dive in eccentric drunken loops
idling around the crown
while darkness steeps the lethal carpet
of sterile leaves,

then go to roost
apart, far from the muscle-bound bronze limbs
towering alone above
a barren circle of distinction
into silence.

CAESAR

Heel planted on the summit of the state
Caesar gnaws his knuckles, pouts and glowers:
in search of enemies with eagle eye
he stabs at the horizon.
What good is power if it does not show?

His partisans wave metal birds on poles
aloft above the heads of the multitude
with flags that droop or stiffen as the wind shifts.
What use supremacy
if it submits to wisdom, virtue, prudence?

Only reckless folly drives it home,
only the naked blade, the raptor's cry
unheard amid the uproar. In the remote
coastal villages ignorant
fishermen will learn to shudder at the name.

DOXOLOGY

Praise monsters if you mean to rise.
Praise them that fatten on their neighbors' hunger
dividing each from each and all from all to make weak prey.
They are above the law because they own the law.
Praise monsters.

Praise clear cutters and strip miners,
praise marketeers of poison and delusion,
manufacturers of scarcity and profiteers of famine.
The earth is their inheritance to desecrate.
Praise monsters.

Praise the single eye that blazes
atop the pyramid where we keep our places
by keeping down those underneath and rise by the betrayal
of those who stand beside us. Praise servitude. Praise fear.
Praise monsters.

Last praise the dust thrown in your eyes.
Throw another fistful for yourself!
Can't you see a brighter future glinting in the grime?
Praise your gag and praise your blinders.
Praise monsters.

POETICS

Identical dime-size disks
represent pupils, with a wedge cut out of each
to index the angle of incidence of hypothetical daylight,
supercilious eyebrows arching symmetrical sockets,
and bamboo-leaf-and-shoot exacto-knife tattoos incised

like broad parentheses
of pure abstraction bracketing plump pumpkin cheeks
around the austere draftsmanship of the precision leer.
The other jack-o'-lantern looks like it was carved
in a hurry by a child with both hands on a too large knife

but notice how haphazard
slashes contrive the sawtooth jaw from disarray
and tilt its crescent gape lopsided under eyelids drooping
drunkenly—no cut wasted, no stroke gone astray.
On a picnic table two jack-o'-lanterns side by side

burning at nightfall,
Parnassian post mod, and psychotic punk.
Trick or treat? The wind shifts, the oak tops rock, the candles
pulsing inside the pumpkins waver and catch, fire
steadying behind the grins, flashing from the eyes.

THE NEW COLOSSUS

A caul of hammered gold obscures her skull:
the ancient spiky crown is shorn away.
A folded circus tent wedged in her jaws
for gag; no blindfold, since the eyes are gone;
her torch winched to a grave among mute fish—
the pedestal is entirely concealed
by tiers of scaffolds; a cross of girdered trusswork
towers behind her like the skeleton
left standing after a skyscraper burns,
with her extended arms pinned at the wrists
to each extremity. She sags forward.
Her neck droops garlanded with massive chains
of stainless steel reflecting on each link
Liberty Crucified by Mammon, Inc.

THE JUGGERNAUT OF THE APOCALYPSE

Rush hour backed up bumper to bumper in all directions
spewing carcinogenic petrochemical smog
the drivers and the driven
bent to the wheel, stalled in toxic buyproducts,
everyone hunched facing the same way:

when the juggernaut of the apocalypse
reaches the brink of the abyss and starts over
in our relentless progress
about to plummet to the final crash
eyes averted in the rearview mirror

the ecocidal maniac behind the wheel
wearing the face of anyone stuck in traffic, fuming,
wrinkles of resentment
from a lifetime biting back sharp words
pinched down tight at the corners of the mouth

meaning to get ahead at any cost and not
let anyone cut in, protected by
a blank look like a mask
as if it were the car that drives itself
through the streets of a city already dead.

NIGHT OF THE COMET

Outside, look, on the table, that sunflower
dry by now, left for days,
crowned with a dandelion halo glowing
star-like by moonlight, rays beaming rays,
caught in the heart

of the flower, its huge myriad insect eye
honeycomb of a thousand cells
plundered by birds. Gone now the sunny pride,
it lies here in its leaves, wilted,
dry as the skin

of the old man sitting this morning in the shade,
head on his hand,
elbow perched at the table's precipice
to support a sleep so deep
not even the sun,

encroaching, wakes him—him that lived ten thousand
days in the glaring fields.
Now in bed, I imagine, with his eyes wide open
he asks himself what is it all for,
motionless as the hills

tonight in silent tribute to the comet
taking its leave without ever
turning its back on the last glow of sunset,
the dazzle of that inescapable
blinding appointment.

Carlo Anceschi

WL 8338

I know a nameless lake in the Sierra
where lunker rainbow rise at every cast
and mating dragonflies
skitter above the surface
and hummingbirds with iridescent eyes.

No trail leads here. No ducks point the way.
Whatever route you find will be your own.
Nearby, it is so quiet
approaching through the trees
the wind is audible minutes away

and when it stills, the water's face relaxes
within its margin of untrodden meadow
and smoothes and clears to show
beneath what's imaged here
the undisturbed reflection of its form.

NEAR BUCKEYE FORKS

It's time I wrote my "bearshit-on-the-trail" poem
though generally in California wild bears
don't defecate on trails. I don't mean garbage-eating camp bears
strung out on junk food plundered from the plastic coolers
of frightened tourists from New York and Massachusetts

or rare imported bears displayed at zoos, bears
dancing in circuses disguised as lapdogs
or stuffed and posed in public institutions. By wild bears
I mean ones mostly never seen besides off-trail.
What need for paths have animals who somersault

through boulderfields and cliff-face willow thickets
unimpeded, like clowns in baggy overalls
practicing gymnastic stunts? Sunny summer mornings
a bear shits in the shade on hemlock duff and sprawls
circles in the meadow, toppling corn lilies like a child.

His ropy coil of grass deposited
out of the wind behind the summit outcrop
means early season is lean enough it makes a bear eat weeds;
ripe huckleberries and fragmented trout bones splattered
on lichened granite lakeside say good times at last.

When a wild bear shits on the trail he means it.
Large fresh piles at emphatic intervals
marking the last mile of descent to Buckeye Forks proclaim
the pocket glade overlooking the confluence
and berry thicket at the ford his personal domain.

SIERRA GENTIANS

Most summers Sierra gentians bloom unnoticed
hidden in meadow grass on their short stems—
a lowly flower the yellowish white of old bone,
its chalices are more conspicuous, their throats
exposed in the sparse grass of a dry year.

Stoop closer and the purple streaks appear
that mark the inner faces of the petals:
kneel in the morning dew and see how they descend
inside the bell and disappear, swallowed in shadow
among a fading speckle of green flecks—

pale trumpets trailing in the sandy soil
at lakeside, tiny bone white cups for Proserpine
gathering dawnlight, humbled in the dirt
where we will all lie down in the one bed together
and each lie down in the one bed apart.

SIEGFRIED'S DESTINY

When Siegfried killed the dragon
guarding the chamber of his destiny,
the mazy cave of legendary echoes,
tasting its blood
he understood

the parlance of the birds
and unperfidious language of wildflowers
and recognized his teacher's wheedling
purposed to wield him
to alien ends

an unknowing tool:
self-deluded in disillusionment,
estranged from his own purposes, astray,
he circled bewildered,
harrowed by furies

that drove him to distrust
even the overdose of dragon's blood
that unstopped his ears to the earth's voices
and purged his wits
of nice lies

delivering him at last
to the high rock-bound narrow windy pass
where the world falls away on both sides, there
to constellate
his fated stars.

ODE ON WATER

ἄριστον μὲν ὕδωρ

Yes, water is best
alive and icy from a free high country creek
or warm from a canteen
overflowing nostrils stinging with sweat
it replenishes the substance

flesh is mostly made of,
the savor of origin surpassing other tastes,
it cleanses and clarifies
the palate and the eyes, renews spirits
flagging when the grade steepens,

it revives desire.
The artificial thunder of military aircraft
penetrates the remotest
recesses and defiles of the High Sierra
banging on the polished walls

of pathless granite canyons
that remain unshaken although the calm is broken
briefly, but when the gods
of weather, by whatever name you please—
Juppiter tonans in excelsis,

ὑψιβρεμέτης Ζεύς,
or Donner der Herr—when the lords of thunder mean
to carve out mile-wide gorges
wearing mountains to sand for Pacific beaches
water is the tool they choose,

water, that always seeks
the depths, following where it's led till its own course
becomes its impetus—
rocketing off boulders into a pool
of candid stillness where trout bask

in shaded pockets, it wells
across the basin's lip to gurgle over cobbles
or cuts lazy oxbows
through a meadow barely whispering
among aspen: always in free

running streams there are voices,
a distant conversation nearly audible
if you listen closely,
its manifold inflections braiding in
a slippery fluent interplay

elusive as Mercury.
These are the voices that consoled Bellerophon
answering his candor
when he wandered in the wilderness
alone, eating his heart out,

hated by all the gods.
At evening he lay down at the water's edge to rest
under the sycamores
and maples, near the meeting of two streams,
and as he drifted off to sleep

among the babbling throng
trying to distinguish the multitude of sounds
entwined in the passing current
and tell each strand by name and character,
he heard them calling amid the clamor,

their polyphony
not to be drowned out by thunder, and they restored him—
a silken curtain sluicing
its mossy slab, the recurrent gulp
of an eddy, a thin drip resonant

in a rock hollow.
So, in early summer when the snowpack melts
in the high country, corn lilies
thrust the speartips of their tight-coiled leaves
up through a snowdrift's thinning margin,

new growth seeking sunlight
to remake the meadow. Every gully swells
with runoff, the least depression
becomes a watercourse as snowmelt finds
its way downhill and where it meets

a trail cut it fills the trench
hikers and horse packers have worn into the soil
and carries off the dirt
and leaves the stones—and, the steeper the path,
the rockier the water leaves it.

TO A SWISS MOUNTAINEER ON SHASTA

You set a stiff pace, Regula,
calves pistoning uptrail ahead.
Slow down. Before dawn yesterday
already halfway up
zigzag stitching switchbacks through the snow

you left the men behind. Below,
they charged the icy slope head on,
stairclimbed twenty steps and stopped,
bent double, breathing hard,
and lunged uphill again like elk in rut

floundering, while you broke trail above them
in methodical traverses,
crampons scrunching crust ice zip zip
like a sewing machine,
summited and descended, passing them still

climbing—and laughed, telling the story
back at Horse Camp, barely noon.
No call to hurry now, though. Look
how long it takes the creek
to make the meadow, slowly layering

bedrock with a sediment
of sand and silt, how many summers
linger in the sunny slab
of turf laid down beside it,
how soft its bed against your dozing cheek.

RANCH HOUSE AT SWARTS

Her peach orchard in flagrant bloom at dusk
spilling its apron of petals above the riverbed
flamingo pink darkening to wine
as evening eases downstream
a prickle of the mountains on the breeze

the intervening yard from her front porch
a labyrinth of junked machinery, wrecked vehicles
stripped, abandoned—this maze of failed devices
like a barricade
distractedly erected by her men

between her and the solitary blush
of color except sage: was it in derision
or from embarrassment? The cool of twilight
washes toward the playa,
her best housedress flaps on the line, damp yet.

TIMON OF PHLIUS

IN THE MUSES' BIRDCAGE

πολλοὶ μὲν βόσκονται ἐν Αἰγύπτῳ πολυφύλῳ
βιβλιακοὶ χαρακῖται ἀπείριτα δηριόωντες
Μουσέων ἐν ταλάρῳ

Many are they who fatten in multicultural Egypt
pedantic cloisterlings waging total war
in the Muses' birdcage.

1.

The Seminar

Eleven crows
eleven strutting crows
studious in a circle
stooped to the gravel
shoulder outside a turn

inquisitive
around the shining meat
of some torn beast, some
indecipherable
crushed small animal—birds

arrogant,
preoccupied: "Fox, or marten?"
"Weasel." "Possum." "Dog?"
Eleven crows
eleven strutting crows.

2.

The Witness

letting it falter
and die away

like water
on coarse sand

leaving the shadow
of its wetness

spilt here
barely a second

3.

The Reader

To be still
as a heron
's reflection's
still, his
bill

tilted up
from the water
to regard
a something
moving:

stilted above
his familiar
rippling double
now shyly
he bends his

knees slowly to sip
attentiveness
at the brimming
verge, now
slips

behind an over-
hanging branch
shyly nipping
insects
one

by one, and perches
on the round of
log above
the water-
line

watching the watcher
through the leaves till
he nods again
above the
page

and slowly while
he's not looking
start to wade
back out
into

the shadowed pond
again

4.

The Hawk

But this was a hawk
in the branches
and it threw
at my true love's feet
for a sign

a bird beheaded,
a limp rag
of blood and
feathers, one
wing

akimbo—and today
a baby mouse
curled in a
bare place dead
on the path,

and that same hoarse
laughter hidden
in the fir
branches clacking
overhead.

5.

The Pond

On the back way
there are planks laid
across the swampy places,
jet black loam where water
pools in the dents,

a place on the path
I double back to
and catch myself returning
mirrored in a sheet
of water, the world

doubled back
in the glassy pool:
wind animates the leaves
and the glint shaken from them
winks flickering

in the pond dreaming
at the secret center
past the last screen
of ferns and creepers, bramble
entanglements

and periphrastic
evasions this place
a steady witness for
the rehearsal of a ghostly
life in signs

and tokens, clairvoyant
the way dreams
betray us to ourselves
in a changeling masquerade
uncovering

another nature
another self
to read in the face there
in the water till reflection
troubles the mirror.

6.

Learning to Drown

> *break on through*
> *to the other side*

to salt a taste
for disaster

I go soliciting
abandon

learning to drown
is what I'm good at

the corkscrew inward
to internal exile

in me my enemy
in my my, in my me

●

that little purple spot
then red then yellow

at the center of the black
behind between closed eyes

that little purple spot
that solar disk in negative

that bruise that hole
that drain consciousness

leaks out of, shimmering
in the inward spiral

●

Sexy Death
now I call you

by your right name
don't deny

I clung for dear
life to your dancer's

body, each muscle
supple as a hand

to greet our need.

7.
Scarcity Economics

The smaller
the pie

the sharper
the knives

the sharper
the knives

the smaller
the pie.

8.

The Image

on a postcard
of Robert Johnson
in a five-and-dime store photobooth
sometime in the '30s, lean

fingers fretting a chord on the neck
of the guitar he holds
between himself
and the camera like protection,
and like a loaded pistol cocked

and pointed. An unlit cigarette
rakes his face. He gazes
steadily, square
into the lens: ready
for anything, unconcerned. Calmly

defying sadness. Behind the canvas
curtain in a whisper
pleading fiercely.
From inside the frame
of light refracted splintering

off the original picture's roughly
scissored edges, he stares out
unflinching in
the sudden glare

9.

The Mayflies

Driving south toward summer
doing 80 down I-5 for hours
into the valley
humid with new corn in sultry rows
for miles and the smell of worms

working in the upturned
earth, thick air surly with burgeoning
and the mayflies
leaving their five-petaled prints like stars
in constellated swarms

across the windshield smearing
the glass with the carnage of my progress
till everything's stained
thin green with insect blood, the controlled
explosions in four

cylinders a frantic
animal lunging against the tether, summer's
hands probing
at the wound to feel the tortured beast
struggle to escape.

10.

My Favorite Metaphor

My favorite metaphor
for suicide
is "checking out"
because it says
here is my key:

the room where I was staying
I won't be needing
anymore
and my departure
proves it's not

a prison: I'm free to leave.
I do. This once
I take command
if in nothing
but this parting

gesture of refusal—and yes,
Javier, yes:
in this life death
is always maybe
only the least

twist away: some slightest
rotation and
you see your hand
x-rayed,
finger bones shining

through the film of skin—
but at 17
in a dorm room
blood welling
from mouth and nose,

already cold in your roommates'
arms—Javier,
Javier, too soon,
too soon

11.

Beauty & The Cripple

Captivated
in our admiring circle
tranced to an ecstatic blank
Beauty's perfect face
collapses seeing

the Cripple enter
and dance his polio
with canes: the specter of the lame
makes Beauty quail, dejected,
abashed to watch

deformity
show grace faltering
under their common burden, alone
in the identical
mirrored cage.

SUBSTRATE

ἀμάρτυρον οὐδὲν ἀείδω

Callimachus

A PAINTED HEMISPHERE

The Mimbres ancients buried family skeletons
prone underneath their pueblo household floors
with broad ceramic bowls inverted over skulls interred
eye sockets upward below their earthen domes,
the inner face a painted hemisphere of art

for blind eternity, a hole punched through the center
of the bowl chosen, fulfilling custom, letting
the breath escape the broken clay, the image, the design.
A lunar rabbit bends a quarter turn
round this one's vacant middle, the winking crow perched halfway

down his backbone beaks the nearest of four pair
of ribs, their cartoon crescents all the remains
of the hare's hindquarters, his waning orb half eaten by the bird
pecking clean the knuckles of his spine—
this fifth moon rabbit, Hare of the May, his good eye cocked

off center at the bottom of a punctured bowl
and grizzled whiskers quiz the solar scavenger
fastened on his shoulder blade, talons in the quick,
in his still gaze outward serenity
a bemused whisper, ". . . sister quail, brother fish . . ."

ALLUVION

Tide pool abalone habitat,
clam beach and mussel rock, reed bed, canebrake,
the terrain tended comprehends a mosaic of
microenvironments,
inland valley oak-and-grassland, foothill chaparral,

sugar pine on the west slope, high, piñon
over the passes eastward thinning out
down desert washes into yucca and agave,
mesquite grove, palm oasis,
each niche a unique interface of common elements

variously configured in pocket climates
from surf to playa hot spring, a four-day walk—
orientation to the sun, proximity
to coastal fog, wind, rainfall,
elevation. Beneficial plants are propagated

in circumjacent drainages to ripen
for harvest in succession. Each favored species
commands a specialist who oversees its use,
conducts its rituals,
chooses a successor—a grandchild, often—and transmits

its store of observation and technique.
Along the edges of wet meadows rushes
for mats and thatching, basket sedges and arrow cane
are spot-burned in three-year cycles.
Pine needles are fired yearly to return their nutrients

to earth and nurse the nut crop. Rocks aligned
in staggered rows oblique to the streambed
when the rare storm issues in freshets at the mouths
of the arroyos slow
and disperse the inundation across alluvial fans to soak,

precipitating plumes of silt downstream
behind them in the shadow of the current.
As the flood recedes these wedges of fresh soil
are broadcast with grass seed
and interplanted with medicinal herbs and salad greens.

DRAKE'S PSALMISTRY

Nova Albion, June 26, 1579

Their king was robed in a coat of coney skins
that reached his waist, and bare besides. Bone rosaries
engirt his shoulders. His crown is a caul of knitwork
covered with a silken down of milkweed seed tufts
that tremble at a breeze

like waves through wheat. His train wears other skins,
the common sort go naked in the nipping colds
that pinch these coasts, their long hair stuck with plumes
behind but in front one only, like a horn, each pleasing
himself in his own device.

When they were nearer all set down their bows
and as men ravished in their minds with fear advanced
wonderingly to worship us as gods.
Mean time the women began to shriek and scratch their cheeks
and bespot their dugs with blood

and dash themselves against the ground in fury
till their strengths failed, no, nor allowed us to hold them back
so mad they were in their Idolatry.
Our General entreated them by gentle signs
to cover their nakedness

gesturing to show we are men not gods
and need to clothe our shame likewise. Our spirits groaned
to see these harmless souls seduced by Satan
and we raised hands and gazed toward heaven to signify
the God whom they ought to serve,

and now we went to reading of the Scriptures
and prayers and singing hymns and they quieted and sat
attentively, with eyes of comprehension
and rejoicing, and at the close of every Psalm
cried with one voice *Hoh!*

       Francis Fletcher

GARCÉS IN ORAIBE   (JULY 3, 1776)

Two leagues southeast I reached a river which I named the Río de San
    Pedro,
the current red and turbid but good water in the pools along the banks.
And six leagues east a town the Yavipais call Muca, which is Oraibe.
Two boys watching sheep and a woman with a hatchet collecting firewood
ran off at my approach.

Poor soil, no pasturage, and stony, but clusters of peach trees along
    ravines
and onions, beans and other garden truck in beds bordering the spring.
Women and children watched me from the pueblo roofs as I dismounted.
The Yavipai, my guide, spoke with one he knew to ask for shelter.
She told him to come up

and to warn me not to—me, nor my baggage either. In a secluded corner
I unsaddled and built a fire of corn cobs in the street and cooked my
    porridge.
Late in the afternoon the men returned with digging sticks and grub hoes
and all day long people were taking looks at me, but none drew close
although I offered shell beads.

Near nightfall an old Zuñi said in Spanish, "Father, these are savages,
who do not wish to be baptized." I held the crucifix for him to kiss.
After dark as people gathered again on roofs around the plaza
a noise of conversation and of laughter, of singing and of flutes
and, after a time, a silence.

A high-pitched voice spoke an oration or a sermon—loud, and very long.
Then talk began again, and quieted. Late that night in the last hours before
    dawn
men strolled about by starlight, quite as in a Spanish town. At daybreak
there was singing in the streets with feather ornamented masks
making an uproar, sticks

dinning against shallow wooden basins and flutes and shouting crowds of
    dancers.
When the sun was finally up the throng surged at me. I feared for my life.
In the lead came the four principal men. The tallest asked, smiling,
"Why have you come here? Don't stay. Go back now to your own land."
I made them signs to be seated

but they did not wish to. I stood up, crucifix in hand, and partly in Yuma,
    partly
in Yavipai, partly in Spanish and with signs, which are the best language,
made known the route my journey followed, the nations I have visited
who passed this crucifix from hand to hand and listened to my words
as now the Hopi also

learning to know the God of Heaven Our Crucified Lord and Savior
    Jesus Christ.
An elder interrupted and answered me in Spanish, his face contorted: "No.
No." "Fetch my mule" I said and, praising their pueblo and their dress,
    and smiling,
rode out past their peculiar houses, neither square nor round, and down
the narrow path off the mesa.

Fray Francisco Garcés

ESSELEN BOWMEN AMONG SAVANTS

La Boussole, *Monterrey, September 21, 1786*

Though rightly our philosophers decry
those circumnavigators who lay claim in their king's name
to newfound lands without regard for the inhabitants
because they come with bayonet and cannon,
Monsieur Rollain, *l'Abbé* Mongès and I

desired to be conveyed ashore this morning
to take possession of this region in the name of *Flora*,
Our Lady Botany. Outside the royal hunting ground
no countryside in Europe so abounds
in game. Pierre and Roux came for the sport

and La Manon pursuant to the study
of savages whom his savants persuade him to call *noble*.
We ranged the hillside southward in botanical researches
and venery. I at once identified
a new procumbent genus of *Pentandria*.

Our ornithologist bagged numerous
examples of the feathered tribe. We will sketch specimens,
dissect and stuff them after sailing. At noon the gray robed Fathers
received us with a sumptuous repast
under an arbor in the Mission garden.

In the adjacent meadow four deer broused,
edging closer by imperceptible increments through lunch
until we recognized natives disguised in hides, their bodies
painted and stag heads fastened on their shoulders.
They pantomime the animal so neatly,

its starts of watchfulness and pauses, feeding—
sighting them unforewarned ten paces off, we would have fired.
This is their stratagem for stalking deer. Often they drop
several before the herd startles and flees.
Through Padre Sitjar we invited them

to join us hunting back to the Presidio.
Firearms no longer terrify them and they are delighted
by the effectiveness at distance of our Fowling Pieces
upon a species of large quail prolific
in coppices, the males with crests reverted,

lead-colored, with ferruginous breast plumage
and pinkish feet, more savory than those of France, and plumper.
Esselen arrows seldom miss and when our fire goes wide
exulting to display superior skill
while yet the birds flare from our shots they bring them down.

       Joseph D'Agelet, Senior Astronomer

FANDANGO

H.M.S. Chatham, *December 3, 1792*

At dusk our cavalcade returned to Monterrey
where Señor Quadra hosted a *fiesta*
in honor of our visit. Society
is small here but it is made large by the addition
of the wives and daughters of the officers

invited almost nightly to the Governor's House.
These ladies know our English minuets
about as well as we know their *borregos*
and this increases the amusement. They wear their tresses
loose at the neck or in long braids, and short-sleeved dresses

leaving the arm bare. Last night's party was to start
at eight; at ten the ladies made their entrance
scurrying by us like the local quail
and settling in a covey on cushions strewn on carpets
over a curious dais facing the ballroom doors.

Sundry dances ensued before the floor was cleared
and a guitar accompanied one couple
in a fandango: sometimes they come close,
veer apart and approach again, wheeling about
and changing sides, smacking their fingers at every turn

with wanton attitudes and leering looks enough
to discompose the gravity of a Stoic.
Captain Vancouver asked our Sandwich Island
passengers to perform a dance and sing
according to their customs. This failed to entertain

one cletch of Spanish women, who seemed to think it meant
for ridicule and departed in a dudgeon.
After the commodore and our captain left
the dancing livened. Male voices joined the choruses
growing more boisterous and discordant as night advanced

from the repeated application of *aguardiente*.
Despite the pious Fathers, native girls
slip from their habitations, loitering
about the woody recesses to catch our notice.
Transparent beads allure and strike them with delight

and earrings gain the favor of the better part.
Rowing back to the ship we watched the stars
begin to pale above the hills and listened
to the guitars and voices carry across the water.
They will keep it up past daylight from the noise.

       Edward Bell, Clerk

THE STAVES

April 13, 1817 — 44°3′ N, 181°8′ W

Confined to cabin through five days by storm off Oonalashka
the expedition's scientific gentlemen
cribbed in the narrow coffins of our berths
continued quizzing Kadu in the dark while heavy seas
lifted the *Rurik* heavenward and pitched her

shuddering from the brink again: Why is the taboo
on men and women eating together not true for fruit?
The answers drifted back like oracles
from the Polynesian's upper bunk. Fruit is a drink.
Why are drums the women's, boats the men's?

Midway from the equator to the arctic pole, bound north
for the Aleutians, a sailor from boyhood, Kadu noted
Sirius setting nightly southward, observed
the flight of birds at dusk and dawn, and could not answer this one,
but when Chamisso asked what the staves meant

carved with notched rings, implanted in pandanus groves, the Kadu
who was seized with shaking to behold a snowflake pause
and vanish on his palm repeated calmly:
What kept the islands' population scanty enough to feed,
and healthy, and long-lived, was ancient custom.

Each child a mother bears after her third she must herself
bury alive. The staves designate burials.
This he attributed insistently
to the scarcity of the islands' parsimonious soil.
We could not help him grasp the concept of life's

continuance after death, he scarcely trusts our accounts of suicides
though history in her book records the self-destruction
of the tribes of the Marianas under Spain—
and still our busy merchant captains rake up the flames of war
to raise their profits on the weapons sold.

     Frederick Eschscholtz, M.D.

BRANDY & CIGARS

Mission San Gabriel, December 11, 1826

Friendship and peace prevail between us and the Spaniards.
I visited their church and saw their molten images.
They have our Savior on the cross, his mother and Mary, the mother
     of James,
and four apostles, all large as life, painted
appropriate to a candy factory.

The men continue quarrelsome and contentious, as since
the expedition left our rendezvous for the Big Salt Lake.
My situation here is delicate, at Father Sanchez's table
in company with the jovial grantees
and dandies of this country in their silks

and ruffles, embroidered vests and silver-buttoned jackets,
I am grotesque seated beside them with soiled pantaloons
and buckskin shirt, and still they treat me as a gentleman and guest.
Tonight at dinner Father Geronimo
dipped his little finger in his wine

and drew maps on the table and kept me talking late
about our route and travels here. I tried to satisfy him
but Mr. Smith was ordered to take our charts along to San Diego
and I was sometimes puzzled in my answers.
Two Indians who act as constables

brought five others to the plaza today at noon
and they were sentenced to be whipped for not working when told.
Each received a dozen lashes on the bare posteriors.
The commandant stood by with his sword ready
to see the one who flogged them did his duty.

They are all older men. Our blacksmiths are employed
preparing nails and horseshoes for our journey to the depot.
This afternoon they finished the bear trap we promised Father Sanchez
and now he pesters me to make him one
to catch the Indians at night who scale

the orchard walls and pilfer in his orange grove.
The padre was quite merry with his brandy and cigars—
though I have seen him throw ripe fruit amongst the younger squaws
        to watch them
scuffle for it. The steward Antonio tells us
the garrison is worried they will rebel

yet for two hours this evening a band of Indians
serenaded us at the priests' door, two violins,
a contrabass, guitars, a trumpet and a triangle. After they stopped,
the soldiers fired a cannonade in honor
of the saint's day tomorrow and together

Spaniards and Indians marched around the mission
in procession. Mr. David Philips, an Englishman,
informs me that the Virgin Mary appeared before an Indian
a year ago and declared this day her feast
and Indians and Spaniards both believe it.

Harrison G. Rogers

THE PELTRIES

on the Klamath and Rogue, 1827

Last night our guides informed us they would separate this morning
and others will conduct us, the cause assigned is apprehension
of being killed on entering the country of their enemies.
The Clamites and the Shastise are at variance near these passes.
If they like war let them enjoy it

and we meanwhile shall wage war with their beaver. Upwards 70
skins to dry, our traps far in the rear, did not raise camp.
This day 13 beaver and 2 Otter   Rain all night.
I sent twelve trappers forward with a guide and 20 horses.
Today's success amounts to seven

Cold night and clear at dawn we started early, a villainous road
and long day's march, worse for the horses, mud, snow in the pass,
we overtook our forward party, descended and encamped
by a small brook. They will raise traps and join us in the morning.
Course this day NW 15 miles

6 men set out at daylight with 60 traps, at eight we ventured
down our brook and camped where it debouches in a basin.
An Indian came boldly to my tent with two fresh salmon.
We have now 30 trappers in advance of the brigade.
No stream escapes our observation.

Sent out my green hands with their gear. *Course NNE 5 miles*
We had a windy night and fair this morning, fine warm weather.
The Indians say the winter is now over. Birds singing,
grass green, and at full growth, flowers—yet it is February.
31 beaver   1 marten

All hands out hunting, in camp the ladies vie at dressing peltry
and drying meat. Today completed our first thousand skins.
We cannot have too many. *Man Is Never Satisfied*
Old Jacques the freeman says three Indians strung their bows at him
and made him signs to leave their land.

He drew the cover from his Gun to give them a salute
when they took flight. McDougal says the Indians break their dams
and make the beaver wild to trap. In shallow water taken
by the forefoot his grinders set him free by amputation.
Traps placed six inches under

catch him by the hind foot, he cannot free himself, and drowns.
The Horse Keeper reports one gone, with saddle, the Company's.
A cold night. Beavers snug inside their lodges, their dams frozen.
Twenty Indians assembled to make peace. Two dozen
buttons settled the affair.

This place is clear of beaver. Four days travel below our traps
the guides are ignorant in all directions further. Last night
it snowed ten inches, at dawn the rain commenced, by now the country
is underwater, the rivers rising. This will not mend the roads.
Louie the Iroquoy found his horse.

          Peter Skene Ogden

COMMONWEALTH

west of the Mississippi, September 1837

The site was cleared and level, the chimney up.
Parties started early felling pines
and skidding back log chains with teams of oxen.
Fresh help arrived all day to join the frolic,
talkative settler wives unloading wagons,

backwoodsmen with their guns and dogs. One man
trims puncheons with an adze and a drawknife.
Others split shingles. Four partner sawing planks
to make the door and a pair of shutters. All
the materials are on the spot by nightfall.

Sunday morning a man with an axe stands
inside each corner of the house to rise
notching mortises to lock the logs
together as we raise them into place
and seat them tier on tier, no trifling task

as the lift up to the top course increases,
yet being many we are equal to it
and the women are abundant with refreshments.
By dusk the walls are up and the roof framed,
the door and window sawn, and we retire

to Collmar's shelter—a fifty-foot screen wall
with a shed roof on poles, three rough-hewn bedsteads,
a loom, two spinning wheels, boxes and casks
for seats, a table, turkey, pumpkin, maize bread
and the frontiersman's favorite beverage, coffee.

The Collmars' new home crowns its knoll, our work,
moonrise pouring through the rafters. They shingle
tomorrow, for Mrs. Collmar is again with child.
Next moon we raise a barn at Slowtrap's. Breakfast
will be frugal: we have eaten everything.

    Hercules Beckwith

AFTER THE RODEO

ἔπεα πτερόεντα

northwest of San Luis Gonzaga, April 1839

We found our horse thieves bathing in the lake
at the foot of the pass. José Bernal, *El Cacalote,*
scouted their camp, slithering like a snake through the *tulares.*
Some were cooking horse meat, others idle.
We circled and surprised them.

The swimmers struggled to climb out and arm
naked, the rest began their war dance, aiming their bows at us,
yelling and grimacing. My brother Bruno rode one down
with his *reata,* noosed and dragged him lifeless
easy as rope a calf.

I spurred for one who volleyed arrows at me
like buns on Christmas Eve. I managed to shoot him in the gut.
He toppled facedown. Cornelio Hernandez ran by shouting
"I'll finish him." The Indian jumped up, let fly,
and collapsed backward. His shaft

pierced Cornelio's neck. He dragged himself
to the corpse, pulled a knife, stabbed, broke the blade between the ribs
and with its stub kept excavating toward the heart, at each blow
croaking "I forgive you, brother" with the arrow wobbling
under his Adam's apple.

Juan Bernal, 1877

WILD MUSTARD REMEMBERS

La Carbonera, Lammas 1842

When no rain fell for twenty-two infernal months
to spare the forage before it failed we tried
stampeding droves of horses over ocean cliffs.
We penned them in corrals to starve. We slaughtered
cattle in numbers surpassing our capacity

to flay or cure the hides and rescue a return
from the disaster by trade with Yankee smugglers.
And still the herds remaining grazed the native grasses
down to the barren root before the feast
of their parched carcasses gorged vultures and coyotes.

And even so, no rain. It was afterward,
once the climate's seasonal storms resumed
their cycle that the alien mustard weed took hold here,
spreading farther north each year. Already
my younger daughters have never seen this countryside

arrayed in March otherwise than in mustard gold.
It grows so rank along the valley bottoms
by May it overtops a person's head on horseback
but, as the summer weather settles in,
hillsides again put on their oaten coat of old

in the weeks when, well before dawn, a warming air
begins to stoke the purgatorial oven
of afternoon. Wisest to rest out the heat
within a cool retreat, shifting from shade
to shade among the oak and aromatic bay

as morning shadows dwindle to a line, a breath,
and pause and change direction while time hangs
aloof, suspended in the balance of the sun,
or from a sheltered cleft gaze out upon
the lion colored landscape with its indecent contours,

the hollows buttocks have, the dimples of a shoulder:
at dusk the deer and cougar disappear
while motionless against its pelt of brittle grasses
when lamps are lighting in the valley's lap
and the emerging stars construct the vault of night.

Guillermo Buckle

THE LANCES OF OLD SPAIN AT SAN PASCUAL

December 6, 1846

With the vanguard of Gen. Kearny's dragoons, frontier scout
Kit Carson, genial cutthroat, collector of scalps,
bearing down at a gallop on San Pascual
by an opportune tumble saved himself
"his horse shot under him"

and lived to tell how they erupted from the chapparal
and charged the California lancer cavalry
—who fled pellmell, and drew them, doubled back
and cut their squads apart piecemeal like cattle
at the *matanʒa,* the razor

reach of Spanish lances from another century
too long for sabers and clubbed bayonets,
desert-bedraggled Army horsemanship
no match for practical *vaquero* mastery
of slaughter from horseback.

Unscathed almost, the Californios retired. Kearny
lost twenty men and could not sit a horse
himself for months. Of those in the first onslaught
only a few stragglers survived the brunt,
the savvy scout among them.

Gen. Pico's victory altered nothing. Kearny was
delayed a week in reaching San Diego.
Old Alta California was still lost,
or won, depending on the point of view.
It was a backward country.

The pennons prancing at the antique lanceheads, the horsemanship
that rivaled Tartary's—style in defeat:
in a half generation two years' drought
and want of capital destroyed the herds
and bankrupted the *rancheros*.

ANNALS OF SAN FRANCISCO (DAYS OF 1854)

The steamships *Yankee Blade* and *John L. Stephens* sailed for Panama
with mail and bullion valued over two and one half million dollars.
Miss Anna Quinn appeared as Little Pickle at the Union Theater.
Squatters ejected from a corner lot at Third and Mission
rioted, wounding George Dillon Smith of the owner's party mortally.

The Rincon Point Schoolhouse was dedicated with imposing
    ceremonies.
A broker named McKinley was arrested swindling in purchases of gold du
J. Gorham Bond, of Boston, drowned while sailing on The Bay.
The people of Drytown strung up a Spaniard for the murder of a
    Chinaman.
A huge new bell was hoisted to the belfry of the Congregational
    Church.

The steamer *Brother Jonathan* departed for San Juan del Sud
with seven hundred thousand dollars worth of treasure stowed aboard.
The ballet pantomime *Red Monster and White Warrior* was brought
    out at the Metropolitan.
A plague of grasshoppers is damaging the crops on the Mokelumne.
The Stevedores and Riggers fête the anniversary of their Association.

347 buildings of 1025 erected for commercial ends
are presently unoccupied due to high rents throughout The City.
The Sons of Temperance and the Cadets paraded Market Street.
Miss Mary J. St. Clair, a necromancer, made her first appearance here.
The celebrated felon known as "Six-Toed Pete" was seized at Saucelito.

The *Golden Gate* docked, thirteen days from Panama with news
of Europe through May 26th and till June 7th for the States.
"General Childs" was jailed for vagrancy and the Recorder
consigned him to reside at the Insane Asylum. The Pilgrim Sunday
       School
assembled at Lone Mountain Cemetery for a children's picnic.

Hughes, the pedestrian, accomplished the extraordinary feat
of walking eighty hours without a stop; the wager was $1,000.
Two men named Frost and Paine resolved a difficulty near the Mission,
the distance forty paces and the weapons Mississippi rifles,
the former shot the latter in the head, causing his instant death.

The dogs infesting Kearny Street were poisoned by an unknown hand,
their dying agonies attracting numerous spectators.
Saloon proprietors met to discuss the abolition of free lunches.
The *Uncle Sam* cleared harbor laden with twelve hundred thousand
       dollars in gold coin.
Lee & Marshall's Circus commenced performing near the International
       Hotel.

JUSTICE TAKES A HOLIDAY

San José, 1861

The settlers meeting at Evergreen Schoolhouse
debated a subscription to buy guns for a defense
in case the Governor calls out the State militia.
After the county posse declined to help enforce the Writ
of Restitution issued by Judge McKee

the League paraded downtown San José
on horseback, friendly, festive, all conspicuously armed,
with the Ladies Auxiliary behind in wagons,
circulating peacefully and paying courteous
visits to merchants who enjoy their custom

before dispersing home, no damage done
save disobedience to the judge's Writ. Many deny
the militia will respond, if called. Others declare
the first shot fired will be the signal for a war on lawyers
with the attorneys for the claimants first to die.

Immigrants from the States are raised to view
unoccupied land as property of their common government
whose policies invite them to settle and improve it
and the vast tracts of unfenced California cattle range
to them appear untenanted and idle

and the immense extent of Mexican
land grants rapacious. To conclude the gathering the ladies
unfurled their Settlers Banner, blue satin lined in white
with silver fringes. One side portrays a farmhouse and the motto
"Resist fraud in obedience to God!"

embroidered in gold thread, the other reads
"The general welfare of the people is the Supreme law."
On May 6th Judge McKee rebuked the bar, adjourned
court for the term without transacting business and departed
for Warm Springs and an extended holiday.

"Touchstone" (for the *Alta California*)

CINNABAR

New Idria, July 24, 1861

The matrix rock is metamorphosed slate, porous, fractured,
the ore distributed capriciously.
Tunnels diverge in all directions threading unmined seams,
the veins of cinnabar diffused in streaks across drift faces
brilliant blood red under our candlelight,

the miners naked above the waist, their shoulders burnished copper,
a hard sort—Cornishmen, Chileans. The mines
are profitable to stockholders. Nine hundred flasks per month
are shipped in pairs by mule for San Francisco. In brick furnaces
the ore, reduced and roasted, distills quicksilver.

The atmosphere it vents of arsenics, sulfurous acids,
and vapors of mercury is ruinous.
The men who go inside to clean the condensation chambers
do not recover, yet the higher wage commands fresh victims yearly,
and all are poisoned by the furnace work.

We reemerged into the scorching daylight world at noon
and took our observations for altitude.
Lunch hour blasting shook our instruments sporadically
like thunder underground, far off, the sand hot through our boots.
North and south from the summit chain after chain

of mountains without one tree, a scene of unmixed desolation,
steep bluffs cut in stratified gravels, hardened,
tilted and stood on edge in recent epoch by earthquake,
eastward across the San Joaquin above the veil of dust
the sawtooth crest of the Sierra glitters.

William Brewer, C.S.G.S.

EPISTEMOLOGY

Eel River drainage, summer 1862

First soldiers ever I see, my lil sister bout three feet high.
Had all Inyan together, gonta takum to Fort Baker.
Mother run away when we hit redwoods. Hide us in hollow tree.
Hear soldier go ways, listen. Go lil further, listen. Dark, them redwoods.
Second night we travel. Out on big ridge at sunup, look over:

Two elk feed by alder spring. Raise up head like tree branches.
Then he run quick. Brush crack way down. We lie there and rest.
Mother begin get sick. She tell us if she die go back to soldiers,
not no other white people. Mother never sleep. I never sleep.
Lil sister sleep. Too tired, lil sister. Next thing, "Children, wake up,
    sunshine."

Get pretty close to bunch grass country, our country. Hear rustle, think
dogs overtake us. Look behind. Skunk family follow us,
mother, five lil ones. Then see soldier hat go by. We drop in fern.
Soldiers catcht us, tookted us to Fort Seward. All our people crying.
White man stand forty Inyan in a row with rope around neck.

Chief Lassik askum, "What this for?" "To hang you, dirty dogs!"
"We done nothing to be hung for. Must we die, shoot us."
So they shoot. All our men. Then build fire with brush and timber
Inyan cut for days and never know they fix own funeral.
Burn all them bodies. Smell raise hair on neck. Make stomach sick, too.

White man come take me South Fork Mountain. His woman got lil baby,
Inyan woman, whip me all time. Didden talk my language.
Nother boy say "Tomorrow white man gonta take you off. Way down.
Better you stay white people, better for you. All your people killed."
So it did happen. I ride packsaddle, blanket over me,

way up Blue Rock Mountain. Dogs bark at gate. They take me off.
Can't walk, ride all day. Woman come out door, I see
she is my people. She know me. She set down on chair, hug me, 'mence cry.
Next morning white man wash my face, count my fingers "one two
        three four days
you going down there, close to ocean." Two Inyan women come.

"Poor my lil sister, where you come from?" "From north. That baldhead
        bring me."
"That way all Inyan children come here." They go. I stand and think.
Nobody here. Only show for me is to run off, now. In kitchen,
take flour sack, loaf bread, matchbox on shelf, big blanket on my bed,
open barn door when I leave, let all horses out.

Rogers my white man come after that. Ellen my cousin's man
worked for him in Hayfork. He took me to take care of then,
that summer. Marry me, too, bimeby, when I get old enough.
Bout size ten girl. I stay long time. My mother come, die there, at Hayfork.
Twenty-five years ago I marry Sam. Marry by preacher.

He's good man. Hayfork Inyan. Talk lil different to us people,
but can understand it. We get old age pension, keep horses, cow,
keep chickens. We live good. I hear people tell what Inyan do
in early days to white man. Nobody say what white man do to Inyan.
That's why I tell it. That's history. That's truth. I seen it myself.

Lucy Young, 1939

TERMS OF EMPLOYMENT

When I was agent for the telegraph
we lost connection on the San Juan to Visalia line
and the front office wired me to restore it.
I rode south up the valley and over Panoche Pass
until I found poles down

then north to Mercy Hotsprings and Los Banos
rounding up the posse of *vaqueros* I hired to help
and with a liberal supply of spirits
to encourage their assistance we completed
repairs expediently

and when I billed the job and itemized
"refreshments $50" they summoned me to San Francisco.
Once I explained and the hi-muck-a-mucks
came down off the ceiling they told me henceforth always
to call liquor "hardware."

Bob Brotherton

ADVENT

I was a grown man when Bogus Tom, Peter, and Shasta Mollie
brought the earth lodge dances. Some folks here spoke their language.
On the way they stopped at every *ranchería*. At Cache Creek
men, women, boys and girls, even children and old blind ladies danced.
The women had their hair down long and crowns of flowers.

Joijoi the Woponuch brought word: "My father asked, 'What kind of
        dance
can you give now, when everyone is dead?' I said
I dreamed the earth is going to be changed and when grass is knee high
the ancestors will rise at dawn and move to meet us from the east.
A wave of north winds and high water will come first

and wash the world ahead of them. Inside earth lodges underground
the people will be safe. The flood tide will roll over
and withdraw. Acorns will be plentiful again. We will live well."
Depot Charlie had one built by fall. The center poles were cedar.
Indians came from Mendocino as far as the coast.

The Warm House was crowded. We circled, men and women alternating
short steps clockwise facing inward. The four dream singers
sat inside with split-stick clappers of elderwood. The Big Head maskers
danced five sets by turns. They had owl down pompoms and
        yellowhammer-quill
headbands with quail plume tremblers nodding from the temples.

People who never danced before did now. Old women danced like girls.
It went on till past dawn. Then we ate, and slept
in the big house half the day. Hardly anyone went to sleep
in his own camp. Everyone was waiting for the world to end.
Most of us wanted to die together in a pile.

We danced four nights and stopped. Some fainted and fell over and
      started dreaming.
There would be no more getting sick and no more dying.
Sixes George said things like that. He lost his wife and son. He shook
all over when he talked, his voice like running water. He stayed with us
for years. He died at Baird about 1902.

The dreaming lasted two years maybe, the dances twenty. Finally the old
dancers died off and the earth lodges rotted away.
Sometimes the town folk would invite the Indians to give a dance
and people used the old time dream song feathers. It was for fun. They
      called it
the Feather Dance. It was mostly a white man's show.

      Coquille Thompson, 1932

SPANISH SONG

The furtive swallows will return
to hang their nests beneath your balcony
and again their flutter at your windowpane
will call you to their play
but those that paused in flight and stayed
to contemplate your beauty and my luck
ah, those that learned our names
ah, they will not return.

The honeysuckle will return
with swelling shoots to climb your garden wall
and again at evening still more beautiful
its flowers will unfold
but those petals pearled with dew
whose droplets we watched shudder
and fall like tears of sunlight,
those, my lady, those will not return.

And to your ears there will return
the sound of words of burning love,
your heart now deep in sleep
perhaps will waken,
but mute, engrossed and kneeling
as you adore Our Lord before His altar
so have I loved you, and don't cheat yourself,
like this, dearest, they will not burn.

Gustavo Adolfo Bécquer

WHEN THE TALKIES CAME TO TOWN

Trombone was my first horn. Proficiency came quickly.
Soon I knew all the brass and most wind instruments.
In those days there were four ballrooms in San José,
each with its orchestra and steady business.
I got my first gig as a high school sophomore

for adult pay, full time. Playing for people dancing
you egg each other on. I was the cat's pajamas.
I'd drive back to the ranch past midnight. Before dawn
your grandfather would wake me to hunt quail,
or deer, or duck. It lasted for six years.

The month the talkies came to town the ballrooms closed.
Folks stopped dancing and sat down in the dark in rows,
listening, in silence, motionless, as in a dream.
A bandmate told me steamship companies
hired musicians. I signed on with Matson

and sailed on the *Malolo,* the pineapple run,
and kept afloat through the Depression traveling
the world with cruise ship orchestras performing show tunes
in grand saloons with rolling decks awash
in anxious wealth. The War put a stop to that.

Too old for war, ashore I started teaching music
in Marysville and Yuba City schools, and after,
enrolled at State for a credential, was asked to stay
as an instructor. When it came time to write
a dissertation I proposed to gauge

our impact on the students' general education
since our State College Charter mandates its promotion.
I tested entering freshmen and graduates and found
we make no difference. My chairman said "Forrest,
you have no problem. Find another topic."

Forrest Baird, D.Ed.

TWO MILLION FEET OF VINYL

San Leandro, 1959

The grinding wheel
requires one hour to ride six feet along its rails
traveling on a sheen of oil
driven by hidden gears. Its spinning rim just kisses
the surface of the vinyl-coated cylinder

clamped in the lathe
rotating slowly in the opposite direction
and every particle protruding
above the calibrated level is sheared off
as it passes, leaving behind a roller face

perfectly smooth
so airbrushed photographs of the cooked colored fruit
are replicated without blemish
and look natural on the labels of canned peaches.
The wheel's abrasive face obliterates all flaws

as it revolves,
the grind removes obtrusive abnormalities,
the cannery press prints clean and true,
no kinks, no smear. Each can of fruit produced entails
a label, labels require printing, and presses need

rollers polished.
One man can tend six lathes. Punched-in on the time clock
six feet an hour for eight-hour shifts
five weekly, forty-eight weeks a year, that's two million
feet of vinyl in a lifetime ground to powder.

Bernie Hernandez

ORION THE HUNTER

outside Los Banos, November 16, 1963

The old man is shouting in the dark "Get up! Get up!"
Outside the cabin, still hours till dawn, the boy's piss
steams in the alkaline dust.
Clear and bright in the sharp November air
the shining path of the Milky Way

arches overhead, and Orion the Hunter, and the Dog.
Out beyond the levee coots cluck in their sleep.
Gas lamps catch and flare
from other cabins. Inside, the old man
has his coffee on the stove.

In the clubhouse by lantern light the men stand in a circle
drawing lots for blinds. Each man gets his chance
to crank the handle, spinning
numbered wooden balls in a wire cage
till one tumbles down the chute

and rolls out. Some men ask their sons to draw for them, for luck.
The old man says to take his turn and when the boy
pulls a middling number
pats his shoulder: they'll split up, pick blinds
outside the main lake, and work the birds

back and forth between them with a side pond to themselves.
The path along the levee is slippery in the dark.
Ahead, the old man waves
a flashlight and curses, laughing, as the dog
splashes after a jackrabbit.

Virgo is climbing toward the zenith, Orion in the west.
The boy wades out into the pond. Its smooth black surface
vanishes in night
against the further shore. The bottom mud
tugs at his boots and each step sends

a long swell rolling outward into unbegotten darkness
sparkling with reflected starlight. He finds the tiny
island where his blind is
by the decoys spread around it, a pair
of buried barrels with iron stools,

and listens to the old man and the dog wade out to theirs.
The east begins to pale. In the band of light
widening on the horizon
a V of sprig is taking off. Already
there are gunshots from other ponds.

A flight of teal veers past the old man's blind. He does not fire
and they continue gliding low above the water,
circle and set their wings
while the boy remembers to keep still
until they come in range.

PAISANO

That was a good end, Frank, clam digging north of Pismo
your old fat body toppled in the surf
slammed to the sand in cardiac arrest,
the golden labrador circling and returning
to nose the sodden corpse—colder each time, stiffer—

a bone damp chilly dawn, low tide, socked in with fog.
Pacheco Pass, back before the war,
one sweet duck gun the Winchester over-under
scabbarded on the fender of your Indian
biking into Los Banos for Basque food and wild ladies:

"opened the cabin door, she stood there just in hip boots—"
Stopped the truck and vanished in the fog
across cow pasture and returned arms full
of portabello mushrooms, a paisano luxury
alongside porterhouses on the grill, potatoes,

the cabin air smoked blind with garlic and fried onions
and California Dago Red and laughter.
The family ranch, 80 acres of orchard
bulldozed for development: walnut, apricot,
cherries—Bings and Tartarians—uprooted, toppled,

overthrown. Clotted with clods, the fists of the root knots
clench skyward, torn, their branches smoking pyres:
the ruffled veil of foam slides up the beach,
the backwash piling up against the dog's paws
splashing and slipping back into the outskirts of the breakers.

OUR MUSIC ON THE SHORE

Today at sunset of the longest day
we set these driftwood boats afloat downstream,
twigs lashed with twine, toy rafts with painted masts
candles guttering at their bows,
decks strewn with flowers.

When the waters rose to engulf the world
set adrift with a stone knife in a basket
pitched and lidded a girl and boy survived
alone of all, the story goes,
to start again

and so tonight amid our boats we launch
a basket also—it holds two grass dolls:
the whole flotilla garlanded and decked
with ferns and feathers drifts out into
open water

till the current catches them and they swing
downriver, candles fluttering in the dusk.
A few will reach the river mouth by morning
gathered into the oceanic
element and dissolved.

ACKNOWLEDGMENTS and NOTES

Gratitude to the editors and acknowledgments to the publications where these poems originally appeared, sometimes in earlier versions:

COMMON KNOWLEDGE: "The Night of the Comet," "Spanish Song"

CONJUNCTIONS: "The Seminar," "The Witness," "The Reader," "The Hawk," "The Pond," "Learning to Drown," "The Image," "The Mayflies," "My Favorite Metaphor," "Beauty & The Cripple"

DOUBLE CONE QUARTERLY (Ventanawild.org): "The Double Altar on Pine Ridge"

FIRST THINGS: "Ancestral Tumulus"

NUMBERS (England): "The Hawk," "The Pond," "The Image," "My Favorite Metaphor," "Beauty & The Cripple"

PN REVIEW (England): "Mimesis," "*Sempervirens* in Winter," "The Wreck of the *Psyche*," "The Seminar," "The Reader"

POESIA (Milan, with Italian translations by Carlo Anceschi): "Rates of Combustion," "Habitat," "First Light," "WL 8338," "Ode on Water," "To a Swiss Mountaineer," "The Seminar," "The Witness," "The Reader," "The Hawk," "The Pond," "A Painted Hemisphere," "Garcés in Oraibe (July 3, 1776)"

POETRY (Oct. 2003): "Caesar," "Doxology," "The Juggernaut of the Apocalypse"

SLATE.COM: "Habitat," "First Light," "The Seamstress," "Temperament," "Sierra Gentians," "Siegfried's Destiny," "Drake's Psalmistry," "Wild Mustard Remembers," "Two Million Feet of Vinyl"

THE THREEPENNY REVIEW: "The Resurrection of the Body," "Rates of Combustion," "Pyramid Scheme," "Sovereignty," "A Victorian Connoisseur of Sunsets," "WL 8338," "Ode on Water," "Ranch House at Swarts," "Cinnabar," "Terms of Employment," "Advent," "Paisano"

TIKKUN: "An Oracle Madrone"

ZYZZYVA: "Near Buckeye Forks"

"Doxology" is included in the *California Legacy Anthology of Poetry*, edited by Dana Gioia, Jack Hicks, and Chryss Yost.

"First Light" is set in type designed by David Lance Goines in porcelain enamel on cast-iron set into the sidewalk in the Poetry Walk on Addison Street in Berkeley and is included in the *Addison Street Anthology* edited by Jessica Fisher and Robert Hass.

"Pyramid Scheme" was published as an ABC No Rio Broadside by Peter Spagnuolo.

I wish to express my appreciation to Wendy Lesser, publisher and editor of *The Threepenny Review*, and to Robert Pinsky, poetry editor at Slate.com.

*

"Habitat": VELENO   NON TOCCARE: "Poison, Don't Touch."

The epigraph of "Exposure" is from "South Coast" by Lillian Bos Ross; Ramblin' Jack Elliott's album *South Coast* includes a performance. In California anywhere there are deer there are cougar, and the deer know it.

"The Seamstress" is for Cynthia Ponce Martinez with the permission of David Martinez.

"Mimesis" is in memory of California painter Oma Perry (1880–1961).

"*Sempervirens* in Winter" is for Natalie and Jeff, Maxine and Miles. Coast Redwood is *Sequoia sempervirens.*

"Vernacular" is for Jack Grosse, for the Lost Dogs, and for friends at the Peak.

"Quill": *inter odoratum lauri nemus:* "within the aromatic laurel grove." Virgil, *Aeneid,* Bk. VI.

"Consolation to a Dancer" is in memory of Jerry Garcia, to Teri Jasman, for the dancers and the dance, from The 418 concentrically outward.

"Poetics" is for Gaelen and Emily Nyokka-Morrell.

"Night of the Comet" is a translation from the Italian of *Notte della cometa,* made in collaboration with the author, Carlo Anceschi.

"WL 8338" is for Greg Muck. On a topographic map WL 8338 indicates that the Water Level of the lake is 8,338 feet above sea level; unnamed lakes are designated in these terms.

"Ode on Water": The epigraph is the beginning of Pindar's First Olympian Ode; my first line translates it. *Juppiter tonans in excelsis* misquotes Horace, "Jupiter thundering on high." ὑψιβρεμέτης Ζεύς: *hupsibremetes Zeus* (hoopsy-BREM-et-ace Zeus), Homer's "high-thundering Zeus." "Donner der Herr": Wagner's Lord Thunder.

In The Muses' Birdcage: The epigraph is Timon of Phlius, Fragment 60 ed. Wachsmuth.

"My Favorite Metaphor" is for J.V. among the dead, and for J.P.D. among the living.

Substrate: ἀμάρτυρον οὐδὲν ἀείδω: *amartyron ouden aeido* (a-MAR-tu-ron OO-den a-AY-doe): Callimachus, Fragment 612: "I'm interested in the poetry of fact" . . . "I sing nothing without witness" . . . "This is a documentary poem." . . . "Don't blame me: it says right here . . ." . . . ". . . as the Booke us telles . . ." (Chaucer) . . . "No fact without a footnote." . . .

"Fandango": I thank Kevin L. Stewart of the Alexander Turnbull Library in Wellington, New Zealand, for providing a copy of a typed transcript of the pertinent passage of Edward Bell's manuscript journal. H.M.S. *Chatham* was part of the English expedition under Capt. George Vancouver exploring and mapping the northwest coast of North America. Bell uses "borego" as the name of a local dance, otherwise unknown; *"borrego"* means "sheep, silly lamb, simpleton," and also "a hoax." Maybe the women of Monterrey were putting on their visitors.

"Brandy & Cigars": Harrison G. Rogers was Jedediah Smith's steward on his expedition to California in 1826–1827. The Virgin of Guadalupe (la Virgen del Tepeyac) appeared to Juan Diego in 1531.

"Wild Mustard Remembers": The title is from a poem by Lorna Dee Cervantes, "Freeway 280" (in *Emplumada*). William Buckle (1803–ca. 1859), an English sailor, landed in Southern California before 1823 and came north after the drought of 1828–1829. He was baptized "José Guillermo" in Monterey in 1829 and married Antonia Castro. Over the next fifteen years they had eight children including five daughters (four by 1840), all at Branciforte (Santa Cruz). He prospered as a lumberman and shipbuilder and in 1838 obtained confirmation of the grant of La Carbonera, at Swanton, Santa Cruz County.

"Epistemology" is derived from the oral autobiography of Lucy Young transcribed by Edith V. A. Murphey and published in the *California Historical Society Quarterly* in December 1941.

"Spanish Song" is a translation from the Spanish of a nineteenth-century California *cancionero* text of the poem of Gustavo Adolfo Bécquer (1836–1870), "Volverán las oscuras golondrinas," commonly called "Las Golondrinas de Bécquer," "The Swallows of Bécquer."

"When the Talkies Came to Town" is in memory of Forrest Baird.

"Orion the Hunter" and "Paisano" are in memory of Frank Cisternino.

I am grateful for the benefit of a fellowship from the John D. & Catherine T. MacArthur Foundation, which materially supported the preliminaries of *Substrate*.

ABOUT THE AUTHOR

Jim Powell is the author of *It Was Fever That Made the World* and the translator of *The Poetry of Sappho* and *Catullan Revenants*. He was awarded a CCLM Younger Poets Prize in 1986 and a MacArthur Fellowship (1993–1998), and was the Sherry Memorial Poet at the University of Chicago in 2005. He is a fourth generation native and lifelong resident of the San Francisco Bay region.

A NOTE ON THE TYPE

This book was set in Fournier, a typeface named for Pierre Simon Fournier *fils* (1712–1768), a celebrated French type designer. Coming from a family of typefounders, Fournier was an extraordinarily prolific designer of typefaces and of typographic ornaments. He was also the author of the important *Manuel typographique* (1764–1766), in which he attempted to work out a system for standardizing type measurement in points, a system that is still in use internationally.

Composed by North Market Street Graphics
Lancaster, Pennsylvania

Printed and bound by R. R. Donnelley
Harrisonburg, Virginia

Designed by Susan Hood